Contents:

GW00383915

The Tao of Laoo

Mr Laoo's guide on how you live life properly

By Fran Kissling

designed by hydesign ltd

I. About Mr Laoo

This Mr Laoo.

Mr Laoo wise man. He know how live life and he also very deep thinker. This why Mr Laoo always very happy. Mr Laoo want share wisdom with other people so they better understand world and know how best to live.

This Mr Laoo's cow.

This cow no know anything.

He lazy cow.

He no read The Tao of Laoo.

He stupid cow.

Here some quotes Mr Laoo put together for powerful self-help book so other people can be more like Mr Laoo and no like his stupid cow.

Mr Laoo no actually from particular place.
He enlightened enough to know world as whole much more important than country. Mr Laoo travel all the time to become even more wise if that even possible!
This mainly no English speaking countries so Mr Laoo no have perfect grammer.

However Mr Laoo no need this.
He connect with people in much deeper way
which you find out when you read book.

When you finish book you see world a bit different.
You realise world actually made of tiny pieces
that together form shape of world. You also no need read other
book again. However many people make
living from books so good to buy anyway.

Now Mr Laoo wish you all the best
with positive transformation.

II. Wise Quotes by Mr Laoo

How to Be Good Leader

"Good leader admit he wrong.
Better leader never wrong in first place"
Mr Laoo, Feb 2015

"You want to be leader. Make sure you have people behind you
going in same direction"
Mr Laoo, Jan 2012

"Good think outside box. Also every other
activity easier if you no in box"
Mr Laoo, April 2017

12

How You No Feel Bad
if You No Good Leader

"Even greatest ruler in world not always
best at measuring"
Mr Laoo, Nov 2004

Important Insights on Universe

"If sun set in west that good omen.
Means solar system working properly"
Mr Laoo, June 2007

"The universe truly big. But could be bigger"
Mr Laoo, April 2011

"We are insignificant compared to universe.
Anyone with low self-esteem probably right"
Mr Laoo, July 2010

How to Know What Truly Exist by Mr Laoo

"There lot of things that exist
but there nothing that no exist"
Mr Laoo, Feb 2013

What Meaning of Life Actually Mean

"You want find meaning of life.
Look in dictionary"
Mr Laoo, August 1998

"You still no find meaning of life.
Make sure your dictionary in English language"
Mr Laoo, August 1998

"You still no find meaning of life.
Get new dictionary. Old one rubbish"
Mr Laoo, August 1998

16

"You think life worth nothing. You tried selling it?"
Mr Laoo, Dec 2014

"You no think you can make difference in life.
Try subtraction"
Mr Laoo, Oct 2010

How You Achieve Happiness Without Tears

"Appreciate small things in life.
They no take up too much room"
Mr Laoo, Aug 2003

"He who only see half full glass
never actually drink"
Mr Laoo, Dec 2017

"You no want feel small.
You stand next to ant"
Mr Laoo, May 2015

"You have lots of obstacles in life.
Build decent assault course"
Mr Laoo, March 2004

"Talking bout feelings no necessary
if you excellent at mime"
Mr Laoo, Oct 2010

"Good try no be jealous. Best have everything
then you no reason to be jealous"
Mr Laoo, Jan 2012

"You can avoid all regret if memory bad enough"
Mr Laoo, March 2012

"No worry bout waist expanding.
Because universe also expanding"
Mr Laoo, April 2011

"You like life in fast lane.
Make sure you drive on right side of road.
Left side in England.
And wear seatbelt"
Mr Laoo, Nov 2003

"Good live each day as if that day last day in life.
But with you no dying"
Mr Laoo, Sept 2008

"You can run away from problems.
Especially if problem angry tortoise"
Mr Laoo, Aug 2011

"To have life you like, like life you have"
Mr Laoo, Jan 1999

"Drinking to forget only work
if you remember to drink"
Mr Laoo, Jan 2013

Mr Laoo's Lessons on Money

"Being rich no mean you happy.
Unless you spend money on Prozac"
Mr Laoo, Feb 2008

"Rich man sometime have as much money as poor man.
Just have different currency"
Mr Laoo, May 2017

"Some people say money make world go round.
That not true. It actually gravity combined
with conservation of angular momentum"
Mr Laoo, Aug 2009

How to be Kind and Why it Important

"Good no hit other person.
You never know if they martial art expert
or something"
Mr Laoo, Sept 2017

"Always show old people respect.
If you lucky they leave you money in will"
Mr Laoo, Aug 2004

"Important you have good heart.
Otherwise you probably get heart attack or something"
Mr Laoo, Nov 2018

"He who no tell truth will get eaten by elephant"
Mr Laoo, May 2017

Cultural respect important.
Never ask extraterrsestrials where they really from"
Mr Laoo, April 2016

"Be kind to cows.
They probably not as intelligent as you"
Mr Laoo, Feb 2015

"Good see things from other peoples' point of view.
Specially if they tall and you in crowd at music festival"
Mr Laoo, Feb 2005

"Always be nice to wife.
Even if she not yours"
Mr Laoo, Oct 2017

How you get Wisdom
(Hint: It Really All Bout Learning!)

"All knowledge you need already inside yourself.
If you choose right question"
Mr Laoo, Oct 2010

"Never forget to remember.
Otherwise you never remember what you forgot"
Mr Laoo, Sept 2005

"Good to grow in life. But make sure you never tall enough to
bang head on doorframes"
Mr Laoo, Jan 2009

"He who drink tea sometime can be wise.
But sometime he who no drink tea also wise"
Mr Laoo, Jan 2005

"To know what you no know. First you need know what you
know. Otherwise you no know"
Mr Laoo, Feb 2011

"He who no read, stupid and no know much
(it ok to write, he no read this!)"
Mr Laoo, Jan 2010

"You want find wisdom.
Better let wisdom find you.
Much less effort"
Mr Laoo, Sept 2001

"Everyone have book inside of them.
Believe me, you feel much better
after it surgically removed"
Mr Laoo, April 2002

"Follow wise man but not all the time.
He sometime go to toilet"
Mr Laoo, Jan 2019

How You Have Big Success Quickly by Mr Laoo

"Sharing problem good.
Though best completely give problem to someone else"
Mr Laoo, July 2001

"If you bread winner good to share bread with others
who no won competition"
Mr Laoo, Dec 2004

"You want be remembered. You need spend time with
elephants"
Mr Laoo, Sept 2016

"Never be afraid of changing.
Wearing same clothes all your life get smelly"
Mr Laoo, Feb 2001

"Yook Aant always get what you want.
Be more like Mr Aant"
Mr Laoo, Mar 1978

"Always good to walk before you run.
Unless you sprinter in competition"
Mr Laoo, May 2000

"You want go far in life.
Get plane ticket to other side of world"
Mr Laoo, Nov 2007

"You want lose weight and be rich.
You sell organs. But Mr Laoo no recommend this"
Mr Laoo, June 2001

"You want be best in your field.
You need become farmer and also have tiny field"
Mr Laoo, Aug 2018

"You want to be winner.
Make sure you only person in race"
Mr Laoo, August 2007

"In life you always need be able to take first step.
If no, you never walk anywhere at all"
Mr Laoo, Nov 2008

"Thinning hair good way to lose weight gradually"
Mr Laoo, July 2010

"Good to live dream.
But better no sleep all the time"
Mr Laoo, June 2009

"He who no on right path should take different one"
Mr Laoo, Feb 2008

"You can do anything you want.
As long as you no too ambitious"
Mr Laoo, Jan 2008

Mr Laoo's Thoughts
on Family and Friends

"You no like family.
Try get adopted by better family"
Mr Laoo, May 2011 *

*Mr Laoo no try this yet
so not 100% sure if this actually work.

"It no important what someone look like,
it what inside a person that matter.
But usually you only see that if you a surgeon"
Mr Laoo, May 2015

"You lose friends easily.
Maybe friends you choose too small"
Mr Laoo, April 2018

"Never talk bout people behind their back.
Best talk bout other people when you really
far away from them"
Mr Laoo, Feb 2012

"It true, race no matter in life.
Only important that you win. Choose race you particularly good
at or where competitors rubbish"
Mr Laoo, Feb 2014

"You want find wife. Look where she last seen"
Mr Laoo, June 2007

How You Find Yourself Quickly and Easily

"To find yourself, you need lose yourself first"
Mr Laoo, Aug 2013

"Finding yourself the easiest thing.
However, if you still no find yourself,
get Sat Nav tracking device on mobile
and keep it with you all the time"
Mr Laoo, Nov 2005

"If you no like who you are.
Be like person you like"
Mr Laoo, Feb 2012

"If you no believe in yourself
maybe you no really exist"
Mr Laoo, Feb 2007

"Keep friends close but enemies closer.
That way enemies easier to kill"
Mr Laoo, June 2009

"You want survive death.
Choose reincarnation if that an option"
Mr Laoo, Oct 2017

"Good walk away from a fight.
Better run away from fight especially
if enemy big and with weapon"
Mr Laoo, Sept 2016

"To win war you need kill all enemies.
And no make no new enemies"
Mr Laoo, Jan 2019

"You want to be great warrior.
You first need learn to fight well.
And have much better weapon than your enemy.
Sometime run away help – but sneak back and
kill enemy when not looking"
Mr Laoo, March 2009

"Violence not always the answer.
It depend on question"
Mr Laoo, June 2001

Wisdom that No Fit in Other Categories

"It impossible in life have too much clean underwear"
Mr Laoo, Jan 2002

"He who purely right wing or left wing
all the time never actually fly"
Mr Laoo, Aug 2011

"If you big headed you probably have strong neck"
Mr Laoo, Feb 2012

"Pride come before fall.
Never be proud on edge of high cliff"
Mr Laoo, Jan 1998

"You only can find inner child
if you have outer adult"
Mr Laoo, Sept 2002

"He who has weak will has strong won't"
Mr Laoo, Jan 2011

"Counting chickens before they hatch only work
if chicken come before egg"
Mr Laoo, April 2009

"He who question everything actually really annoying"
Mr Laoo, Feb 2019

"She who try to hide behind smile
definitely get found"
Mr Laoo, Dec 2014

"He who no live in present
may have his future in past"
Mr Laoo, July 2082

"Turns out sometime people no live in present
cause friends very stingy and present too small"
Mr Laoo, July 2021

"Good to be patient.
But much better you no get ill in first place"
Mr Laoo, Nov 2002

"Good remember dead people.
Then you no do same thing that make them die"
Mr Laoo, March 2009

"If you no can be free in life,
at least try no charge much money"
Mr Laoo, Oct 2003

How to No Feel Bad
If You No Live Life Well
by Mr Laoo

"He who never truly live life also never truly die"
Mr Laoo, Feb 2005

Dear Mr Laoo,

I have just started living in the university halls and unfortunately my culinary skills are somewhat lacking. How long does it take to boil an egg?

Yours sincerely,

Marjorie White

Dear Marjorie White,

Question depend on many things. Canary egg no take as long as egg from ostrich. Method you use for boiling also important. Also depend how high up you are. You on top of high mountain, water no take long at all to boil. Also if you in space, this completely change situation. Life not always simple and boiling egg also part of life. Be more specific bout situation and ask question again.

May your life always be successful and you get double doctorate if that possible.

Mr Laoo

Dear Mr Laoo,

I've been in love with a woman from my office for five years now but she doesn't seem to know I exist. I'm too shy to speak to her and but I can't go on like this. What's the best way to connect with her?

Any help with this is hugely appreciated.

Unlucky in Love

Dear Unlucky,

First you need make sure you definitely exist and you not actually ghost who think they alive or something. If you really actual person you can write letter or even send E-Mail to her.
Most offices have E-Mail and stationary so that not actually a problem. Make sure she know you really exist and have ID ready to show if she need proof.

May you get promoted at least five times and you never have boring meeting.

Mr Laoo

Dear Mr Laoo,

I'm not sure what to do. I'm completely bored of life and nothing seems to have a meaning anymore. Is there anything you can do to help?

Sad

Dear Sad,

Everything have meaning. Start slow, looking up words in dictionary. Then go to sentences. Finally read complete Tao of Laoo. Then everything have meaning and nothing boring at all. You wonder how you live life before Tao of Laoo and tell everyone they need read this book so their life as good as yours.

May you win every battle you fight in and may any clothes you wear look good on you.

Mr Laoo

Dear Mr Laoo,

I have recently been appointed as the leader of a large country. I'm sad to report that it hasn't been going well. The economy's terrible and I've been made an object of ridicule in the press. I'm trying to make everything work but there's so much involved in running a country and because of how my political system works, it is very hard to get anything done.

Do you have any recommendations on how I can successfully lead my country and keep my sanity at the same time?

Best Wishes,

Tough Being President

Dear Tough,

Large country particularly hard to manage. Have you thought bout letting other country invade some of yours so you have less work? Lots of countries out there looking for more territory. Some very friendly and will treat people well. If you give new leader Tao of Laoo they understand how to be best leader possible. Once you only have small country to manage you can take lots of holiday and make big difference with much less effort.

May you never accidentally eat rotten food and may you always have friendly pets.

Mr Laoo

Dear Mr Laoo,

I have been a Bhuddist for 15 years now but am now unsure as to whether I have chosen the right path. Sometimes I have doubts bout my spirituality. What should I do?

Yours,

Crisis of Faith

Dear Crisis,

If you have map and compass you can tell if you on right path. If still no help, do orienteering course. Mr Laoo looked up Bhuddism and that real religion. You no need doubt it. If you Bhuddist for 15 years you really should know that. Study religion harder so you at least know little bout it.

May you have many followers and win every competition you enter.

Mr Laoo

Dear Mr Laoo,

I'm afraid I'm in a bad place at the moment as my wife has just left me taking the children with her. I really don't know what to do. Can you help me?

Upset

Dear Upset,

Having place to yourself best time to have party. Invite everyone. You have good music and wine people no care too much if your place bad. Air freshener can make big difference though.

May you be famous and many people jealous of you.

Mr Laoo

Dear Mr Laoo,

I'm a city trader and have just accidentally lost my company fifty million dollars. I will most likely lose my job and may possibly face time in prison.

What shall I do?

Desperate for Help

Dear Desperate,

You know where fifty million ended up? Join that company, they really love you there and treat you like hero. If you lucky they get you decent lawyer so you no need go to prison.

Read Tao of Laoo, specifically Mr Laoo's Lessons on Money, so you get better feeling for money and no make financial mistake in future.

May you always find good bargain and may people laugh whenever you make joke.

Mr Laoo

IV. Mr Laoo's Personality Test - How Much Like Mr Laoo Are You?

1.) You see man who upset because he no pass exam.
Do you:

A.) Say that a shame. He need try harder next time.

B.) Give him The Tao of Laoo so he have more wisdom to
pass or even if he no pass, he no feel too bad bout it.

C.) Tell him bout how you pass exams and what
important in life cause ~~you are Mr Laoo.~~
I mean cause you very wise person.

2.)   You no very happy, what do you do:

A.)   You feel sorry for yourself and eat lot of ice cream.

B.)   You read The Tao of Laoo and feel lot better.

C.)   This situation never happen cause you always
        very happy.

3.)   Someone ask you if The Tao of Laoo good book. You say:

A.)   I no heard of The Tao of Laoo.

B.)   I read it and it best book I ever read.
Everyone need read it.

C.)   I wrote The Tao of Laoo and it excellent book.
Everyone need read it.

4.) Person ask how similar to Mr Laoo you think you are.
You say:

A.) No even know who Mr Laoo is. Who is Mr Laoo?
He same person who write Tao of Laoo in question
you ask before?

B.) Think me quite similar to Mr Laoo and of course
very happy bout that.

C.) Me actually same as Mr Laoo.

Answers:

You get mostly As – you look at 1.

You get mostly Bs – you look at 2.

You get mostly Cs – You look at 3.

1.)   You not at all like Mr Laoo.
       You need read book properly again to understand
       ways of Mr Laoo. If you no can read good try get
       audio tape or something.

2.)   You a bit like Mr Laoo.
       You understand book but always good try to be
       more like Mr Laoo to lead best life. Tell friends bout
       Mr Laoo so they too have better life.

3.)   You are Mr Laoo.
       That no possible. There only one Mr Laoo!!! This only
       true if me fill in questionnaire and you know you no
       really me!!!

V. Mr Laoo's Wishes to Reader at the End of Book

Now you finish reading Mr Laoo's words of wisdom and
you know how best live life. If you follow ways of
Tao of Laoo, you too can be more like Mr Laoo.

Mr Laoo now wish you all best on your journey through life.
May health and happiness always be with you.
And may you be rich and have many friends.

Mr Laoo

THE END

Printed in Great Britain
by Amazon

82145553R00047